Friends Afloat

Story by
Eliza Rosenbaum

Illustrations by
Jean Pidgeon

RSVP
RAINTREE
STECK-VAUGHN
P U B L I S H E R S
The Steck-Vaughn Company

Austin, Texas

To my third grade teacher, Mrs. Penny Benjamin, for an unforgettable year
filled with magic, fun, and excitement. — **E.R.**

To Jean Bradley (my mom) with love. — **J.P.**

2 3 4 5 6 7 8 9 0   RRD   97 96 95 94 93

Library of Congress Number: 92–39029

Library of Congress Cataloging-in-Publication Data

Rosenbaum, Eliza, 1983–
  Friends afloat / story by Eliza Rosenbaum; illustrations by Jean Pidgeon.
  p.   cm. — (Publish-a-book)
  Summary: Eight animals on a sailboat learn that by using their individual
talents for the good of the group they all benefit and keep each other afloat
and safe.
  1. Children's writings, American.   [1. Cooperativeness — Fiction.
2. Boats and boating — Fiction.   3. Animals — Fiction.   4. Children's
writings.]   I. Pidgeon, Jean, ill.   II. Title.   III. Series.
PZ7.R71876Fr   1993   [Fic] — dc20   92–39029

ISBN 0-8114-3584-9 hardcover library binding   CIP
ISBN 0-8114-7776-2 softcover binding   AC

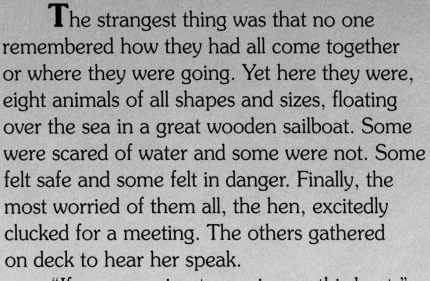

The strangest thing was that no one remembered how they had all come together or where they were going. Yet here they were, eight animals of all shapes and sizes, floating over the sea in a great wooden sailboat. Some were scared of water and some were not. Some felt safe and some felt in danger. Finally, the most worried of them all, the hen, excitedly clucked for a meeting. The others gathered on deck to hear her speak.

"If we are going to survive on this boat," said Hen, "we need to help each other and ourselves by sharing and cooperating."

"But how?" interrupted Mouse.

"Well," said Hen sternly, "if you don't interrupt me, I'll tell you."

"Well, sorreee . . .," squeaked Mouse.

4

"**A**s I was saying," clucked Hen, staring angrily at Mouse, "each of you will have a job. I have it all planned out. Giraffe, where are you?"

"Right here," said Giraffe.

"You are going to put up the sail and help look out far over the ocean to see if land is near, okay?"

"Okay," said Giraffe.

"Eagle! Come down off that mast!" The great bird flew down to her. She clucked loudly, "You, Eagle, will fly ahead to the closest island to get hay for Elephant."

"I'll do the best I can," said Eagle.

"Good," clucked Hen. "Penguin, your job is underwater, patching up the boat and catching fish. It's a big job, but I think you'll manage."

"Sure," gulped Penguin.

"Cricket, where are you?" called Hen. "Can you chirp a little so I'll know where you are?"

"Sure," chirped Cricket. "Chirp, chirp."

"Oh, there you are," exclaimed Hen. "Cricket, you will play beautiful music to keep our spirits up. You have a little job, but it's important," she added.

"I'm glad to have that job," chirped Cricket. "I love making music."

"Perfect," said Hen as she looked around. "Oh, Mouse, your job is to make repairs in small places where no one else can fit."

"Okay," squeaked Mouse.

"**N**ow let's see. . . . Ah, yes, Elephant, you don't need to tell me where *you* are. You need to use your trunk to pump out water that could sink the boat."

"Okay," said Elephant. "I'll do my very best."

"Monkey, you're next. You alone have hands, so you can fix things and steer the boat."

"Got it, got it," chattered Monkey.

"As for me, I will lay eggs for everyone to eat, call meetings, and be the leader. Is that okay?"

Everyone shouted, "Yes!"

"Let's all get to work," said Hen, and she went off to lay eggs.

The next morning, all went to their jobs as usual. The sea appeared peaceful, but just that day a horrible, mean old sea-king, who hated everyone and everything, saw the bottom of the boat floating over him and was furious.

"Trespassers!" he yelled so loudly that Cricket and Mouse felt the boat rumble. He summoned a great storm.

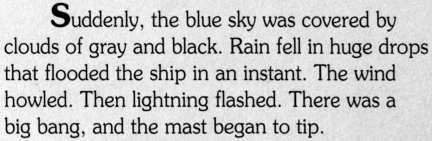

Suddenly, the blue sky was covered by clouds of gray and black. Rain fell in huge drops that flooded the ship in an instant. The wind howled. Then lightning flashed. There was a big bang, and the mast began to tip.

"Elephant!" cried Hen. "Start pumping water out of the boat, and fast!"

"Right away!" shouted Elephant, and off he stomped.

"**M**onkey, steer the ship," ordered Hen. "Eagle, fly high above the clouds to see which way the storm is coming, then tell Monkey which way to steer."

Monkey and Eagle rushed off.

"Giraffe!" ordered Hen. "You will be our mast. Hold up the sail in your mouth so that we can keep sailing. Cricket, play music to calm everybody down."

"Yes, ma'am," chirped Cricket, and off he hopped. But the wind was too much for Cricket, and he was blown overboard.

Hen called to Penguin, "Dive in and try to find Cricket — fast!"

Penguin dove into the water and saw something wiggly floating by. "Cricket!" she thought, but it was only seaweed. But the next seaweed had six skinny legs sticking out. She scooped up Cricket.

Back on the boat, Penguin saw Hen
tangled in rope. No one there could free her.
Penguin shouted, "Where's Mouse?"
Mouse came quickly and chewed the
rope to free Hen.

They kept sailing, guided by Eagle. All at once, the sky cleared and there was a beautiful rainbow. Everyone was silent.

At that moment, Cricket chirped, "I know why we are all here. The boat is now our world. We don't need to know how or why we got here. We only need to keep afloat and keep each other safe by cooperating and sharing.

"We're all good at something," Cricket continued. "We can help our world and ourselves by working together to keep the boat sailing forever."

Eliza Rosenbaum always had encouragement for writing from all the teachers at her beloved Cabot School in Newton, Massachusetts, where she is a fourth grader. The school, from kindergarten on, strongly supports creative thinking, reading, and writing. In return, Eliza celebrated her winning story by reading it to a special school assembly on a day the mayor proclaimed "Eliza Rosenbaum Day" in her honor.

Eliza's creative efforts get continual practice in the service of entertaining little brother, Blake (age three), who hangs on her every word. Eliza also has followed in the footsteps of older brother, Jed (age twelve), in her love of reading, writing, music, and sports. When not absorbed in books, she may be found practicing the piano, representing Newton on a soccer travel team, or playing with her good friends Audrey and Hannah. She dreams of one day being a writer, artist, or pianist, but maybe also a professional soccer player.

She confesses her favorite food is candy (almost any) and her favorite place to be in the world is the island of Nantucket where she spends time each summer with her brothers, mother Lidia, and father Jerry.

© Art Illman Ph

The ten honorable-mention winners in the **1992 Raintree/Steck-Vaughn Young Publish-a-Book Contest** were Cody Hill of Portland, Oregon; Matthew Mizdail of Fleetwood, Pennsylvania; Sarah Stair of Knoxville, Tennessee; Claudio Astorino of Hazleton, Pennsylvania; Courtney Withey of Rexford, New York; Jamie Pope of North Zulch, Texas; Jared Halpern of Azle, Texas; Olivia Esh of Lewistown, Pennsylvania; Mira Carrberry of La Habra, California; and Brooke Doyle of Memphis, Tennessee.

Jean Pidgeon was born in Baltimore, Maryland, and has been a freelance illustrator since 1975 when she took a leap-of-faith and started her own business. In the last several years, she has specialized in illustration for children and is delighted with her new niche. She feels blessed not only to be earning her living, but also to be having a great time in the process. She lives in Pasadena, Maryland, with Michael and Tilly (the rabbit).